FOREWORD

Quite why I should have been asked to write this Foreword is a mystery to me, but I jumped at the chance. As this series identifies, Wales truly is a different country, one which cares about its past, its language and its cultural traditions; one in which myth and legend are deliberately entwined with historical fact to emphasise its separateness from the large and influential mob next door. History, both ancient and modern, applies a revisionist assessment to its principal actors; heroes are defrocked, villains are sanctified, zealots and flag-wavers are judged anew for the worthiness of their cause. Such is the stuff of history, and the more so in Wales where myth and legend have greater status.

Saints and sinners abound in Welsh history and mythology and retain an influence on modern Welsh life which, for good or ill, has been largely lost in the rest of Britain. This reluctance to let go of history means that in Wales the past is not another country, it is a fundamental and continuing part of the country and no one can pretend to understand what makes modern Wales tick without at least a nodding acquaintance with some of the principal characters who have shaped events in Wales.

The lives of the famous saints revealed here show the often cult-like influence of early Christian missionaries, and the deliberate carelessness with which later chroniclers have chosen to record their deeds in order to magnify their impact – for whatever purpose suited at the time, as the life of St David so clearly demonstrates. It seems that the practice of not allowing the truth to get in the way of a good story has a long and discreditable history, but it is a tactic that works, as the existence of this very book proves. Latterday saints such as Bishop William Morgan, in large measure personally responsible for the survival to the present day of the Welsh language, are of surer record and greater influence, and no less fascinating.

Sinners often hold even more fascination than the saints; we all love a story of bad behaviour. It is a remarkable fact that the passage of time renders even so foul a pirate as Hari Morgan a sort of cult hero, his life lionised in celluloid. Strict historical accuracy seems to matter as little with sinners as it did with the early saints – a message that resonates down the ages and can be seen to be influential in contemporary society.

This book offers an interesting insight into Wales's past, looking entertainingly at some of those who have shaped the country and people that we see today. I commend it to you, and look forward to my own entry in a future edition.

Richard Brunstrom
Chief Constable
North Wales Police

D0528870

Saint Brynach –

Talking With Animals And Angels

… at his command wild beasts set aside their brutal habits, and were rendered tame … he led a life so pleasing to God that, as he deserved, he enjoyed frequently the sight and discourse of angels …

(Medieval biographer)

St Brynach on Carn Ingli

A saint's fame and cult status is often denoted by the occurrence of wells and places named after him in a particular geographical area. In north Pembrokeshire there are churches dedicated to St Brynach at Nevern, Dinas, Pontfaen, Llanfyrnach and Henry's Moat. Several wells bearing his name in isolated valleys and by lonely pathways pay homage to this Irish hermit who struggled to found a Christian community in what was clearly a wild, pagan stronghold in the sixth century.

His arrival in Wales was almost accidental. Legend tells that he sailed from Brittany on a rock bound for Ireland, but was diverted, by God's will, up the Cleddau estuary to Milford Haven. There this handsome man caught the fancy of a nobleman's proud daughter who, when her advances were spurned, sent a servant to spear Brynach under cover of darkness. Brynach escaped, (but the servant didn't, for from the wound he inflicted on this godly man, flying ants appeared and stung his attacker to death). Brynach bathed his wounds in a spring nearby, which forever after flowed red. Hence its name, Ffynnon Goch. (A well in Llanfair Nantgwyn parish has that name and might well be the very place where this incident 'happened'. As late as 1665 Court Sessions records referred to a field near Trefach as *Parc y ffynnon vernach*.)

Against this background of hostility and anti-Christian tradition Brynach is said to have settled in the Gwaun valley, where he set up a small monastic hermitage on the banks of the Caman brook, a tributary of the river Nyfer. Such was his relationship with nature and with his Creator that he was able to stand upon the nearby Preseli hills and commune not only with the birds and animals, but also with God's messengers – thus giving the nearest mountain its name, Carn Ingli, the Mount of Angels.

Celtic cross at Nevern

One of the most famous legends attached to St Brynach is centred upon the arrival of the Nevern cuckoo, which every spring came and perched on the impressive Celtic cross close to the church door, and then invaded the nests of hedgerow birds. Every year, Brynach celebrated a special mass on its arrival.

One particular spring the congregation waited and waited, becoming more and more agitated and unbelieving, as the feathered visitor failed to show. Brynach refused to begin his service. Then, late in the icy afternoon, a fluttering was heard outside the door, and a single 'cu ... koooo'. The mass went ahead. As the celebrants left the church rejoicing, there on the path, beneath the carved cross, they found the freezing lifeless body of the cuckoo. It had indeed returned from warmer climes to welcome the Welsh spring – but the journey had proved too much for Brynach's faithful bird.

There are, as often occurs in legends, chronological discrepancies in this heart-rending tale – since Brynach and his followers predate the cross by several centuries.

st. brynach's church

henry's moat

eglwys y sant brynach

Saint Melangell and Saint Silyn

Saviours of the Forest

Above: Silyn's protection of the stag
Right: Painting of Melangell by Jen Delyth

Melangell is one of the most famous Welsh women saints — and the story of her protective powers have become a part of folklore. Originally from Ireland she had settled in the Tanat valley. One day she was startled in her prayers by a hare which rushed to hide in the folds of her cloak. It was being pursued by the hounds of Brochel, Prince of Powys. He was so moved by Melangell's concern for the helpless creature that he promised her and the trembling creature protection.

She later became Abbess of a small religious community, which over the centuries became, and has remained, a place of pilgrimage. Pennant Melangell, set in the heart of the Berwyn mountains, is built within a Bronze Age site, ringed by 2000-year-old yew trees, and has been totally restored within the last twenty years as a centre for pilgrimage

Much less well known is the Carmarthenshire hermit, Silyn, near the site of whose ancient cell a tree was bedecked with rags until the early nineteenth century. The scraps of cloth represented the votive offerings of Gwernogle village folk, remembering age-old traditions of the saint's healing powers, and replicated today by children hanging prayer-leaves onto bare branches in Sunday school activities across the world.

Yet Silyn and Melangell have much in common, for both had animal companions, whose lives were threatened by the outside world — by materialistic princes and noblemen who misunderstood the natural harmony between saint and creature. Silyn gave protection to a hunted stag, and this event is linked to the Welsh name for a plant called Buck's Horn Plantain — *Llysiau Silyn*, or Silyn's herbs.

Welsh Hares First Hunted Now Protected

It's the hare that we go hunting
On a fine and windswept day,
From the gorse she's just been flushed out –
Dogs and cats are gone away.
Just like the wind, or even swifter
After the hare and hounds we ride,
Dodging through the upland sheeptracks
Of our native countryside.

traditional

Though hunting the hare is now illegal, intensification of lowland agriculture and decline of natural habitats such as woodlands and uncultivated fields has contributed to a general decline in the brown hare population in Wales. But Biodiversity Action Plan programmes are encouraging efforts to more than double their numbers to around 2 million in 2010. Wildlife Trust members have recently reported hares on the sand dunes at Harlech, Cors Goch nature reserve and Halkyn Mountain.

*Above: Melangell stands up to
Prince Brochel
Below: Pennant Melangell Church,
a centre for pigrimage*

SAINT DAVID –

DO THE LITTLE THINGS THAT YOU HAVE SEEN AND HEARD IN ME

Statue of St David at Llanddewibrefi

Stories of St David abound, but few of them are based on fact. His major biographer and source of reference was Rhygyfarch who was writing about David five centuries after his death, in his *Buchedd Dewi* ('The Life of David'). He was actually constructing a well-balanced propaganda machine to ensure that the See of St David's in the far corner of Pembrokeshire remained highly regarded, and, if possible, outstripped Canterbury, and became autonomous as the centre of Welsh Christianity.

Perhaps for this reason Rhygyfach embellished some of the known facts about David's life – such as his miraculous ability to bring sight to the blind Paulinus, and to raise the ground at Llanddewibrefi to make himself visible from afar.

Despite these newsworthy events, the favourite images of the saint for many are those of the earnest monastery pupil, by legend son of Sant, King of Ceredigion, and Non, granddaughter of Prince Brychan, who grew up to respect nature, and all the little things of life. His reputedly simple life, and his choice of settlement in the beautiful, sheltered Glyn Rhosyn, which we now know as the cathedral city of St Davids, has endeared him to millions of pilgrims and worshippers for over a thousand years.

Although Canterbury's importance remained supreme in the Anglican church, particularly after the martyrdom of Thomas Beckett, David's fame and his Christian leadership continued to be celebrated. His monastery became a place of pilgrimage for Norman and Plantagenet kings and princes and after his canonisation in 1120, and the rediscovery of his grave in the mid-thirteenth century, was second only to Rome and Santiago de Compostela in the hearts of repentant sinners. Indeed a variety of written sources and proclamations by popes and chroniclers make it clear – in an early form of travel propaganda – that twice to St David's equalled a single pilgrimage to Rome.

Seek St Davids twice if you wish to visit Rome
Equal merit will be given to you here and there
Rome gives once as much as St Davids gives double.

from

A Song of the Western Road

The road to old St David's
  Is the white road of the Blest,
The olden road that brought the vales
  The palmer's songs, the pilgrim tales,
When all the wandering roads of Wales
  Went winding to the west.

The road to old St David's
  Is a road that has no end,
A road of legend and ringing rhymes
  Of splendid songs and singing chimes;
A road where every pilgrim climbs
  To God as to a friend.

A G Prys-Jones, H.M.Inspector of Schools, 1925

In the eighteenth century St David's Day began to be celebrated as a national festival, and since then millions of schoolchildren have dressed up in 'traditional' costume, to mark the patron saint's special day. Daffodils and leeks have become the national emblems; daffodils – known as Peter's leeks, *cennin Pedr*, in Welsh – because they flower in springtime, close to March 1st, St David's Day, and leeks because David, during times of prayer and fasting, apparently lived for many months on wild leeks and clear spring water.

He did onlie drink what crystal river yields
And fed upon the leakes he gathered in the fields
In memory of whom in the revolving year
The Welshman on that day that sacred herb doth wear

Below left: children visit the cathedral at St David's
right: St David's Day celebrations at Gladstone
Infants School, Cardiff, 1931
bottom: St David's Cathedral, Glyn Rhosyn

St. DAVID of WALES

With lifted hand St. David blessed the bees

One tale of David's simple kindness and consideration for others concerns St Domnoc and the bees. Domnoc was an Irish monk who settled at Glyn Rhosyn, working in the kitchens and the monastery gardens. His passion was bee-keeping, and he worked hard to build up the number of hives: they provided honey as a sweetener and an ingredient for mead, and wax for altar candles. After several years Domnoc became homesick and prepared to leave Wales. However, each time he got into his boat at Porthclais the bees swarmed and followed him. Frustrated, he asked David what he should do. The abbot merely smiled, blessed the bees and said 'Take them with you – there are many more than we shall ever need.' So Domnoc sailed across the Irish Sea with a swarm of bees. And that, so the stories goes, is how the first bees reached the Emerald Isle.

Saint Winifred

. . . AND SEVERED SAINTS

Saint Winifred's Well at Holywell in Flintshire is indeed one of the holiest shrines in Wales, and one of the oldest too, since a fragment of an eighth-century reliquary known as *Arch Gwenffrewi,* or Winifred's Casket, was found there, proving that the beheaded maiden was regarded as a saint almost immediately after her death, around 650 AD.

Apparently the young maiden, a novice nun of noble parents, was pursued by Prince Caradog, who attempted to seduce her. When she fled to the monk Beuno's church for sanctuary, the prince caught her and struck off her head. Beuno picked up the head and gently replaced it on the mutilated body. Winifred was restored to life through his prayers, and her assassin was subsequently hunted down by her brother Owain and killed in revenge.

Hers was, in fact, not an unusual story, since many holy wells in Wales bear witness to the awful fate of maidens who were attacked for their piety, their beliefs or, more commonly, their good looks. St. Lludd was one such victim. She was chased down Slwch hill in Breconshire by her assassin, and where her severed head came to rest against a boulder *a Cleare Spring of Water Issued out of the Rock.*

Men's heads too produced streams of healing waters. Justinian carried his head across the sea from Ramsey Island to the Pembrokeshire mainland, and Decuman travelled even further, from Somerset to the same Welsh county, tucking his head under his arm. St Decuman's Well still flows near Rhoscrowther church on the Cleddau estuary.

Throughout the Middle Ages kings, princes and lords visited Winifred's shrine on pilgrimage, or acknowledged its healing properties. A church has stood upon the site since the eleventh century. During the Welsh Henry Tudor's reign the present ornate shrine was built, in late Perpendicular style, under the patronage of his mother Margaret.

Above and left: 'St Winefride's Well' at Holywell
Right: Stained glass window in the small well chapel

SANTES GWENFREWI   SANT BEUNO

Catherine of Aragon's coat of arms are also carved in stone within the shrine itself. Although during the Reformation the status of the well diminished, as Catholics were persecuted, it remained for centuries a place of faith and healing, and after the Catholic Emancipation Act of 1829 enjoyed a revival, becoming known as the 'Lourdes of Wales'.

For hundreds of years people have continued to bathe in St Winifred's Well, and to kneel on St Beuno's steps, where he promised his niece that anyone coming to the well and asking for her blessing 'might receive an answer to their request at least at the third time'.

Until the 1960s the crypt was filled with abandoned crutches and splints, a testimony to the healing powers of the waters – or the enduring faith of its visitors in Gwenffrewi, the seventh-century Welsh nun.

The well in its Gothic building, Holywell

'St Winefride of Wales' painted by American artist Meryl Osse

Richard M Jackson, writing of a weekend excursion in North Wales in the summer of 1820 described the scene as follows: 'Many crutches, wheelbarrows that have supported Invalids to the Well are left there, in remembrance of the great assistance they have derived from bathing in its waters.'

Jinny Jenks, who visited the area in 1772, was shown an ancient oak tree in the middle of a meadow, which supposedly grew from an acorn dropped in the dung of St Winifred's famous Dun Cow, 'during her abode in this farm one night on her journey to St Winifred's Uncle, [Beuno], an old Abbe who liv'd in a Monastry at a great distance, to whom she sent this Cow as a present for the great kindness he had done her, in joining her head at that distance by his prayers.' Apparently the 'country' people from whom Jinny had heard the legend, 'implicity believed' it, and the place took its name, Hafodunos (meaning 'one night's refuge') from the amazing cow, which in one milking produced enough milk to make a ton of cream, as payment for its overnight shelter, and a miraculous gift from Winifred!

MERTHYR TYDFIL AND THE MARTYR TYDFIL

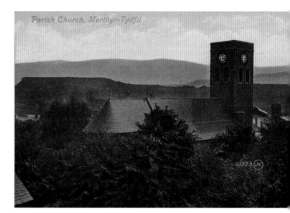

Parish Church, Merthyr-Tydfil

The simple church, within which Tydfil was thought to have been buried, has been rebuilt several times, in the thirteenth century, in 1807 and in 1894. When the Norman church was demolished, two stone pillars and a stone coffin built into the foundations were unearthed. Perhaps this contained the remains of the simple maid who was prepared to die for her faith, and whose saint's day is celebrated on August 23rd.

When the two names are placed side by side the connection seems obvious but few outsiders know the legendary origin of this famous valleys' town, synonymous with the industrial heartland of Wales. Travellers in the nineteenth century described it as 'the greatest mining place in Britain', and the capital of the iron and coal industries. George Borrow on his grand tour of Wales in the summer of 1854, revelled in its Satanic character:

> *The town is large and populous. The inhabitants for the most part are Welsh, and Welsh is the language generally spoken, though all have some knowledge of English. The houses are in general low and mean and built of rough grey stone. Merthyr, however, can show several remarkable edifices, though of a gloomy, horrid Satanic character. There is the hall of the Iron, with its arches, from whence proceeds incessantly a thundering noise of hammers. Then there is an edifice at the foot of a mountain, half way up the side of which is a blasted forest, and on the top an enormous crag. A truly wonderful edifice it is, such as Bos would have imagined had he wanted to paint the palace of Satan…*

Wild Wales George Borrow

Many centuries before, it had been a place of refuge and quiet contemplation on the banks of the Taf, 'one of the most beautiful of rivers', and the chosen home of Tydfil, a holy woman, and members of her family — or so the fanciful tale goes. (Actually Tudful could well be a man's name, and *merthyr* could be interpreted as 'shrine').

Tydfil's family tree reads like a medieval volume, *Lives of the Saints*. Her father, half Irish and half Welsh, was Brychan, Prince of Brecon, named Brycheiniawg or the Breconian, who lived in the fifth century and was related to many of the early Celtic Christians who flourished in that time which was to become known as 'The Age of Saints'. He had numerous children, (reputedly 11 sons and 25 daughters) by a variety of wives and concubines and without exception they appear to have been 'saintly' siblings. All were well educated and went to school in Gwenddwr on the Wye. Tydfil was at the centre of a small religious community, building a *llan* or enclosure which contained a tiny wattle and daub church, a hospice and a scriptorium. There she lived, healing the sick and nurturing the Christian beliefs of her followers.

Many of the children's names are almost forgotten – Nennoca, Endelienta, Tanglwstl and Illudiana – but a few, such as St Dwynwen (the patron saint of lovers) and of course Tydfil are still remembered in place-names. Non, the mother of St David himself, was a granddaughter of Prince Brychan.

Legend relates that the aging Brychan, making one last vist to his holy daughters Tanglwstl, at Hafod Tanglwstl and Tydfil, in the Taf valley, allowed himself to become separated from the protection of his son Rhun Dremudd and his grandsons. This provided an opportunity for both groups to be attacked by a marauding band of heathen Saxons, or more probably a Scottish Pict raiding party which had settled in nearby South Radnorshire. Tydfil and three of her brothers, including Arthen, were slain – and ever since that time the place has been called Merthyr Tydfil.

Could the town football club be inviting defeat by calling themselves 'The Martyrs'? Or perhaps they deserve success by their loyalty and defence to the saint who gave their town its name.

The Llanddona Witches

Siani Bwt

Although today it's a tucked-away tourist attraction on the east coast of Anglesey, Red Wharf Bay was once the scene of an Irish invasion. Its effects have never been forgotten. A boatful of strangers, bedraggled women and their menfolk was washed up on the creek, in a hole-riddled, open boat, with neither sail, oars nor rudder. They had escaped a watery grave in the Irish sea, which was probably what their persecutors had intended, but received an equally cool reception from the local fishermen, who suspected they were witches, swept onto Llanddona beach by the incoming tide. The locals tried to drive them back into the sea, but one woman with more powerful magic than the rest struck the sand – and from there fresh water gushed out in a fountain. Either impressed or bewildered, the villagers agreed to let the families stay – provided they made their camp well outside the village.

And stay they did – frightening the natives into submission; the women never paid for anything and the men, with their distinctive red neckerchiefs, made a living by smuggling – releasing deadly black flies from their scarves when the going got tough, or the Customs men challenged their authority.

There were two particularly famous witches – Bella Fawr and Siani Bwt. Big Bella is linked in legend with the farmer Goronwy ap Tudur – the only local man prepared to stand up to her scheming ways, and able to counteract her magic, whether it be with ground adder skins to sprinkle on bewitched farm animals, churchyard earth to cover his cottage floor or silver bullets rather than shot to fire at her (since a witch's flesh is apparently impervious to lead). Many of Bella's tricks involved shape-shifting into a hare's form, or preparing cabbalistic verses on her visits to the cursing well at Menai Bridge.

Finally Goronwy gained the upper hand – sticking pins into a doll made from an oak-tree fungus known as witch's butter, and calling out Bella's name.

Exidia glandulosa, *a slimy black jelly fungus nicknamed Black Witch's Butter, grows on rotting or dead oak trees.*

She was forced to pronounce a blessing on him, his family and his livestock, and he was never troubled by the Llanddona witches again.

Siani Bwt (Short Betty) bore several of the standard hallmarks of 'the witch'. She was diminutive in stature (44 inches tall) with raven black hair – and had two thumbs on her left hand. Presumably they twitched, like those of the witches in Shakespeare's *Macbeth*. They say that her descendants are still in Llanddona.

Saint Dona's Church, Llanddona was founded in the early seventh century, in remembrance of Dona ab Selyf ab Cynon ab Garwyn ab Brochwel, who had built a hermit's cell on the seashore. She is remembered on November 1st – all Saints Day. The present church, with its stunning views of Red Wharf Bay, was completely rebuilt in the mid-Victorian era, and yet remains a place of Celtic spirituality and estuarine peace.

The Witches of Llanddona

These strangers came drifting to Red Wharf Bay
In boats without oars from a land far away
And Anglesey's history was changed that day
   By the Witches of Llanddona.

They were weak and dying from hunger and thirst
Yet the Welsh folk stepped back at the women's curse
As running clear water from the salt beach burst
   Round the Witches of Llanddona.

At damp Fynnon Oer, there was shrieking and moans
As they chanted their curses, for breaking neck bones,
Making men wander over step, stile and stones
   Past the Witches of Llanddona.

So never outbid them on market day,
Never complain when the curds turn to whey,
Never betray them to Excise men's pay,
   Those Witches of Llanddona.

Red Wharf Bay

BIBLES FOR ALL
FROM WILLIAM MORGAN TO MARY JONES

To Bishop Morgan for his pains
We must give thanks the most,
For putting into Welsh the Book
With the strength of the Holy Ghost

(Thomas Jones, vicar of Llandeilo Bertholau, balladeer)

Bishop William Morgan as portrayed by artist Keith Bowen

When William Morgan completed his Welsh translation of the Bible in 1588 it was indeed a great day for the common people of Wales, Until then they, and the priests themselves, had had to rely upon Hebrew, Latin or English texts, which they didn't all understand, or which were commentaries on the scriptures – rather than the Bible text itself. Added to this, many Welsh-speaking priests just didn't have the vocabulary of the Bible, with its unfamiliar references and turns of phrase. A major argument against a Welsh translation was, of course, that it was important for everyone to learn English! William Morgan's response is captured in his cutting declaration, 'In the meantime the people of God will die of hunger for His Word.'

It was while he was vicar of Llanrhaeadr-ym-Mochant that Morgan started his translation. Although much of his time was spent in village quarrels, which became increasingly acrimonious, he was able not only to write his scholarly work, but also to oversee its

printing and publication in London. This was an essential part of the project, since Welsh-speaking editors and proof-readers were few and far between in 1587, and a close watch needed to be kept on the printsetters themselves.

The translation made William Morgan famous. He was an excellent preacher and his fame and skills soon reached the church authorities who, with Elizabeth I's approval appointed him as Bishop of Llandaf.

From his base near Chepstow (the Llandaf palace had been laid waste by Owain Glyndŵr) William continued his writing, revising the text of the New Testament and re-editing the book of Common Prayer for republication in 1599. William Morgan later became Bishop of St Asaph.

Tŷ Mawr, Wybrnant where William Morgan lived as a child, was originally a 16th-century cottage, or perhaps even older, since the central crucks may date back to the Middle ages. Now in the care of the National Trust, it was restored by

Tŷ Mawr Wybrnant

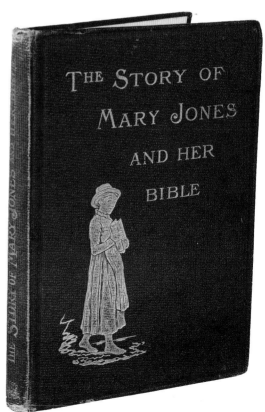

to distribute here and abroad. Griffith Jones from Llanddowror in Carmathenshire set up his famous Welsh Circulating Schools around 1737 to provide opportunities for ordinary folk to actually read the Bible. He argued that many families had Bibles – and revered them as family heirlooms and registers of ancestry – but few were able to read them.

Bible study at home followed this literary awakening, and was further encouraged by Thomas Charles, the charismatic Methodist minister who had settled in Bala after defecting from the Established Church. He made sure that the Sunday schools had plenty of bibles, he published *Trysorfa Ysprydol*, the first Welsh Christian magazine, and he provided an encyclopaedia of the bible, a kind of eighteenth century concordance called *Geiriadur Ysgrythurawl* to help the students, both young and old, who flocked into churches and chapels to read the Word of God for themselves.

And then of course there was Mary Jones, who with her Bible, or with her want of one, has become synonymous with the quest for scriptural knowledge and the right to read. She had learnt her letters at

Lord Penrhyn in the mid nineteenth century, and has become a place of pilgrimage for both theological scholars and those interested in the vernacular architecture of a traditional stone-built Welsh uplands farmhouse and the life of its most famous inhabitant.

Although the Morgan family were poor by some standards, (John ap Morgan being a copyhold tenant to the richer Wynn family from nearby Gwydir) they were descended from high-ranking gentry, and could apparently afford to give their second son, William, a university education which, of course, with his perfect mastery of the Welsh language, made him eminently suitable to take up the challenge so eagerly awaited by those thirsting for the scriptures in their native tongue.

So began a roller-coaster of interest in, and publication of, Bibles in the Welsh language. The 1588 copies had been both expensive and heavy, valuable tomes often chained to church walls and lecterns. Two Welsh merchants living in London, Thomas Myddelton and Rowland Heilyn, backed the production of a smaller, lighter, cheaper version in 1630. They commissioned a print run of five thousand copies of *The Little Bible, Y Beibl Bach* at five shillings a copy – a book truly for the common people.

By the end of the seventeenth century there had been a number of new editions, some encouraged by the newly formed Bible Societies' wishes for texts one of Thomas Charles's circulating schools in Abergynolwyn, and regularly read her neighbour's Bible. Wanting one of her own she saved for six years until she had the three shillings and sixpence needed to purchase one from Mr Charles. Tradition says that the fifteen-year-old girl walked barefoot from her home at Llanfihangel-y-Pennant to Bala, but when she arrived, the preacher's cupboard was bare – the copies ordered from London had not yet arrived. However he was so moved by her determination and spirit that he found lodgings for her in Bala until the books arrived. And then he sold her three for the price of one! As a result of the encounter Thomas Charles was moved to found the British and Foreign Bible Society in 1804 – to ensure that anyone, anywhere in Christendom and beyond, would have access to scripture. Charles himself edited the first Welsh edition published by the society.

Mary later married a weaver, Thomas Lewis, and lived and died in the village of Bryn-crug, near Tywyn, where her cottage and her grave can be seen to this day. There is a monument, too, in the ruins of the cottage where she grew up at Llanfihangel-y-Pennant .

Two of the bibles given to Mary Jones are still in existence; the third has been lost. One is in the

National Library of Wales, and the one which she actually used, and which contains her own writing is in Cambridge University Library.

The British and Foreign Bible Society published a book about Mary in 1882, eighteen years after her death. A sticker on the endpaper shows that the copy shown on page 21, published in 1904 and containing a number of illustrations, was presented by the Society to a Mary Humphrey of the Westholm Girls' School Juvenile Association.

The Song of Mary Jones

They say that Mary Jones was so excited by her purchase, that she sang hymns all the way home to Llanfihangel, and even made up a verse of her own.

Yes, at last I have a Bible,
Homeward now I needs must go:
Every soul in Llanfihangel
I will teach its truths to know;
In its dear treasured pages
Love of God for man I see;
What a joy in my own Bible
To read of his great love for me.

Above: Mary Jones's bible, housed in Cambridge University Library
Below (left): monument to Mary Jones at Llanfihangel-y-Pennant
Below (right): her grave in Bryn-crug

Twm Siôn Cati

And the Highwaymen (and Women) of Wales

O n his walking tour of Wales in 1854, George Borrow met an old drover on the road to Tregaron, and heard first hand the tales about Twm Shone Catti, 'a great man and clever thief' who was born there.

'And what became of him?' said I; 'was he hung?'

'Hung, no! only stupid thief hung. Twm Shone clever thief; died rich man, justice of the peace and mayor of Brecon.'

'Very singular,' said I, 'that they should make a thief mayor of Brecon.'

'O, Twm Shone Catti very different from other thieves; funny fellow, and so good-natured that everybody loved him – so they made him magistrate, not, however, before he had become very rich man by marrying great lady who fell in love with him.'

Often referred to as the Welsh Robin Hood, Twm Siôn Cati is without doubt the most famous outlaw in Wales. There is, however, some confusion over his identity, for by day he led a law-abiding life, as Thomas Jones,

a respectable gentleman and landlord, well-known for his love of history and local genealogy. His exploits, so joyfully narrated by the drover, have been recorded in a variety of forms, from newspaper strip-cartoon to biography, and from 'children's classic' television to rap poem and school musical. Most tend to be based on his adventures as presented by T.J.Llewelyn Pritchard's *The Adventures and Vagaries of Twm Shon Catti*, published first in English in 1828, and later in Welsh. The Welsh version has a little rhyme on its title page, in Welsh,

> Mae llefain mawr a gwaeddi
> Yn Ystradffun eleni
> A cherrig nadd yn toddi'n blwm
> Gan ofn TWM SHÔN CATTI

which suggests how everyone, even the stones themselves, crumbled at his name. His night-time hideout was supposed to be in a cave overlooking the river Tywi between Tregaron and Llandovery. Apparently it is still there – but very hard to locate!

T. Llew Jones, much-revered author of children's books, based a bestselling trilogy on the adventures of Twm Siôn Cati and 'Y Ffordd Beryglus', the dangerous highway

The *Western Mail* newspaper in Cardiff serialised a daily cartoon strip about Twm Siôn Cati in the 1940s. He appeared as a young swashbuckling hero, with a canine companion called Bob Tail, who encountered a variety of villains on the highway, including the wicked Diamond Dan.

The adventures were subsequently published in booklets which sold for a shilling per copy.

There were plenty of stories for children to enjoy, and great scope for the cartoonist. One of the most popular was of Twm's visit to an ironmonger's shop in Llandovery to buy a cauldron – a pot for his porridge. The ironmonger showed him several pots but Twm was not particularly impressed. The ironmonger declared that no better would be found in the kitchen of a king! Twm, holding one of the pots up to the light, said 'There's a hole in this one.' The ironmonger took the pot to inspect it, whereupon Twm flipped it over the poor man's head. 'You tell me, then,' he joked, 'if there is not a hole in it, how have I put such a big stupid head inside it?'

The cartoons which first appeared in serialised form in the Western Mail

This woodcut by E Salter from the 1872 Welsh-language version of Pritchard's 'Adventures' shows Twm selling back to a farmer, Mr Powell, a chestnut horse which he had stolen previously and painted grey. The farmer was duped into buying the fine grey horse at Llandovery market – and did

not discover the deception until the weather changed and it rained, washing the paint away! Similar deceptions occurred at Newton near Brecon, with a stolen bull and a fine false tail, which Twm attaches to its short stump.

Many historians are exceedingly uncomfortable with the legendary status of Twm. One antiquary from Newport, Kyrle Fletcher, wrote in *The Western Mail* in 1922: 'In serious history where we find the real Twm Shon Catti, he is styled "Thomas Jones of Fountain Gate" in Tregaron. His home was a charming old house built out of the ruins of an old Hafod ... and here in his study he had collected a vast store of Welsh manuscripts and rolls of arms ... It is only fair to rescue the reputation of this scholar ... He probably did some foolish things when he was young. Well! Haven't we all done the same?'

Although there were obviously other villains patrolling the highways and byways of rural Wales none have been recorded in such detail. William Davies of Wrexham, known as 'The Golden Farmer',

was supposedly a famous highwaymen, but his story has been lately disproved as the fictional invention of one Captain Alexander Smith, the eighteenth-century author of *The History of the Lives of the Most Noted Highwaymen*. He gave the nickname of a robber called Bennet executed in 1690 to a burglar called William Davies, hanged in 1689 and then created a Welsh identity for him, saying he'd been born in Wrexham in 1627. No proof at all!

Similar unfounded legends surrounded the site of an old oak tree blown down in 1965 at a crossroads close to Plas Noble House near Erddig. It was supposed to have held the gallows where Reynolds, 'the last local highwaymen to be hanged from a tree, in about 1790' died, and beneath which he was buried, hence the local place name 'Reynolds' Grave'.

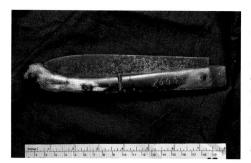

This knife was once thought to belong to Twm Siôn Cati himself, for carved on the one side is the name T JONES, Tregaron, and the date 1606 on the other. In 1911 it was described as such in a Carmarthen Antiquarian Society magazine However, after examination at the Royal Armouries in London it was declared to be a fake – since knives of that type would have been unknown in Tudor times. A Victorian schoolboy prank perhaps, or a local historian's hoax!

One more famous highway person, about whom there is some hard evidence is Einir Wyn, or Madam Wen of Anglesey. In the rocks by Llyn Traffwll there's a cave known as Madam Wen's cave. People say that it has a secret underground chamber, where the notorious highwaywoman stashed the booty which she stole from unsuspecting travellers. There are unconfirmed sightings of a woman swimming across the lake's surface, particularly on Easter Sunday. Could this be the restless ghost of the same Madam Wen, who had once been a wealthy Royalist heiress, whose family's lands and fortune were captured by the Roundheads during the English Civil War? Tradition records that Einir Wyn, determined to restore the family's fortunes, took to a life of crime, smuggling and stealing with a band of fearless accomplices. She had her own ship for smuggling, and sold untaxed goods from her base in Cymyran Bay.

One familiar legend, told of many highwaymen before and after Madam Wen, features a chase across the snow-covered Anglesey countryside. The Excisemen were hot on Madam Wen's trail, following the horse's tracks in the snow. Little did they know that her supporters had re-shod the horses, so that their shoes pointed backwards. The trail led the highwaywoman's pursuers round the island in circles, back to their starting point.

Rhosneigr Bay: one of the legends is of Madam Wen's ghost seen riding across the beach on horseback

HARI MORGAN –

BUCCANEER AND BARBECUER!

Hari Morgan

Henry (or Hari) Morgan's outrageous attacks on the Spanish colonies, especially Panama, brought him fame, fortune and a knighthood from Charles II in 1674 – and the governorship of Jamaica. Although supposedly under license, and with some form of royal assent, this most famous of Welsh pirates tended to make up his own rules of combat. In 1668 his 800 followers attacked the town of El Puerto del Principe on Cuba, defeated the local garrison and forced the men to surrender – by threatening to physically tear apart their wives and children. Henry Morgan also sacked Maracaibo, Venezuela and Portobello, in attacks which relied upon surprise and speed, and involved both sea and land raids.

But life was not always plain sailing, and often times were hard. A *no prey, no pay* system of rewards existed according to contemporary commentators.

And it is recorded that in 1670 Morgan's crew were so hungry that they ate their own manbags! One of them even wrote out the recipe.

Slice the leather into pieces, then soak and beat and rub between stones to tenderise. Scrape off the hair and roast or grill. Cut into smaller pieces and serve with lots of water.

Such a dish might well have made a change from *hard tack*, those weevil-infested, long-lasting ship's biscuits which became the staple diet for a life at sea.

Buccaneers, or illegal seventeenth-century privateers, took their name from the word *boucan*, a kind of smokehouse barbecue used by the Arawak Indians to cure the meat of sea cows (manatees). Legend says that the *boucaniers* invented the cutlass, the long knife for cutting meat which might be held between the teeth of every self-respecting pirate chief. The buccaneers, who began by supplying ships passing the island of Hispaniola (now Haiti) with fresh meat, animal fat and skins, gradually became sailors themselves, creating a 'Loyal Brotherhood of the Coast' and attacking the hated Spaniards. They obeyed no laws but their own, and were renowned for their cruelty: Hari Morgan was no exception. One of his favourite forms of torture was lighted matches under fingernails!

Accounts of the buccaneer's life were first recorded in true accounts of the period, such as *Bucaniers of America* by Alexander Exquemelin (1684), and in the years since, many legends of Hari Morgan's exploits have been retold in stories and films, including John Steinbeck's first novel, *Cup of Gold*. Most swashbuckling of these are Rafael Sabatini's rollicking tales – *Captain Blood,* (1922) *The Chronicles of Captain Blood,* (1930) and *The Fortunes of Captain Blood* (1936), filmed in 1950.

Ballad of Henry Morgan

This is the ballad of Henry Morgan
Who troubled the sleep of the King of Spain
With a frowsy, blowsy, lousy pack
Of the water rats of the Spanish Main,
Rakes and rogues and mad rapscallions
Broken gentlemen, tattermedallions,
Scum and scourge of the hemisphere
Who looted the loot of the stately galleons
Led by Morgan, the Buccaneer.

Berton Braley

Another famous pirate was of course the Welshman Bartholomew Roberts, known as Barti Ddu, or Black Bart (1682-1722). He was 'forced into piracy' when his own ship was captured, but he gave as good as he got – notoriously capturing 400 ships. His Jolly Roger flag featured him drinking with a skeleton!

JEMIMA NICHOLAS

'THE WELSH HEROINE'

Nowadays we might find it hard to believe that an invading army could mistake a gaggle of pitchfork-waving irate women in red shawls and black bonnets as a regiment of British troops – but apparently that's what happened in Fishguard town on a cold February morning in 1797.

A French attack should have been centred upon Bristol, but bad weather forced the fleet westwards and the decision was made to berth in Fishguard harbour. There would be little threat of resistance in that remote, windswept corner of Britain, and besides the Welsh were thought to be anti-Royalists, ripe for revolution! They must have thought 1400 French troops could easily overcome the volunteer militia force – less than a quarter of their number.

However, the enemy was not prepared for Jemima Fawr, Big Jemima – a hard-living, hard-drinking, pipe-smoking, middle-aged cobbler, well known in the *Royal Oak* for her strength and size. While many of the townsfolk abandoned their homes and shops and fled to the surrounding countryside, Jemima is said to have called together her friends, ensured that they were all dressed in their traditional red woollen shawls and black bonnets, and marched towards the beach, brandishing pitchforks and other agricultural implements.

from 'Jemima's marching song'

Get rapping on the windows,
Get tapping on the drums,
Get your shawl and get your hat
Before the French Invasion comes.

It's seventeen-ninety-seven,
They've sailed round the coast of Devon,
Now they've spied the Land of Heaven
In the distance.
They've seen a sign for Abergwaun
And they think that they'll be fine
But they've reckoned without mine
And your resistance!

Black hat tall,
Scarlet shawl,
Pitchfork 'n' all,
We're out to have a Ball . . .

Everyone a redcoat soldier,
We couldn't be much bolder,
Standing shoulder to shoulder
On our road to victory . . .
with . . .
Jemima! Jemima!
In her costume (Designer)
No words can yet define 'er
Courage and 'er glee.

'The Women Soldiers of Fishguard'

Jemima's adventures have become a vital part of Fishguard's folklore, and are often used as a focus for tourist interest, as this illustration from a 1922 publication, *Legend Land*, demonstrates, it 'being a collection of some of the Old Tales told in those Western Parts of Britain served by the Great Western Railway'. The story is also brought to life for walkers in a mosaic laid into the Parrog or sea-front, overlooking Fishguard Bay.

Whether, indeed, they did look like King George's Redcoats is questionable – but it was enough to frighten the ill-disciplined Frenchmen, many of whom were drunk from their late-night looting of the neighbouring farms. Jemima captured twelve soldiers, and marched them back to the town, to a heroine's welcome. Confidence was restored, and by the time British reinforcements arrived, the invading army was in disarray – and eager to call a truce.

Someone back in London believed the story, and Jemima was awarded an annual pension of £50, which she collected every year until her death in 1832, aged 82 years. A memorial stone was erected on her grave 'by subscription collected at the centenary banquet July 6, 1897'. This can be seen in St Mary's churchyard – a fitting tribute to 'JEMIMA NICHOLAS, of this town, The Welsh Heroine who boldly marched to meet the French Invaders.'

To celebrate the 200th centenary the women of Fishguard, led by Elizabeth Cramp, designed and created a 100 foot long tapestry telling the story in stitches of the Last Invasion. Said to rival The Bayeaux Tapestry, and embroidered using specially dyed wool, it is currently on show in the town's public library. This section portrays the capture of twelve French soldiers by Jemima Nicholas.

Twm Carnabwth

A village vigilante

Thomas Rees, or Twm Carnabwth as he came to be known, was a bit of a bruiser, and more than a bit of a boozer! And yet his name has become synonymous with the rights of the common man, for he was almost certainly the infamous 'Rebecca' who first led the riots in Efailwen in May 1839 – a rebellion by small farmers and agricultural workers against the extortionate taxes imposed on road users during very hard times.

Thomas Rees was an agricultural labourer in Mynachlog-ddu who had owned a tiny cottage, Treial, built in a night, close to Glynsaithmaen farm, where incidentally the first meeting of the Rebeccaites was held. By the time of the 1851 census the cottage had been extended and was known as Carnabwth – hence Rees's nickname, Twm Carnabwth (Tom Stone Cottage). Besides being a hard worker the red-headed Tom was also something of a Jeckyll and Hyde. He was renowned for his fists and with a warming drink or two inside him would take on, and usually beat, all comers in booths and impromptu boxing rings at country shows and hiring fairs. Yet he was also a religious

man; his recitation of the *Pwnc* – a form of scriptural catechism – was eagerly awaited each Whitsunday morning at Bethel Chapel in Mynachlog-ddu. Not afraid to stand up to his masters even by day, if he thought his neighbours were being badly treated, and certainly ready for night-time mischief and horseplay, Twm was just the man to lead a gang of righteous rebels. And lead them he did, right to the gates of Efailwen, the first toll-gates to be destroyed.

Some say that these lowly workers were 'put-up to it' by the larger farmers, who paid their tenants and labourers a going rate for appearing in women's clothes at particular gates on particular nights. This may well be true, but it can never detract from the image of the first Rebecca leader, well versed in scripture, well able to recite the lines from Genesis mentioning Rebecca – they became a rallying cry to the impoverished country folk, for whom the breaking of the gates was a just cause.

And they blessed Rebecca and said unto her, 'Thou art our sister, be thou the mother of thousands of millions, And let thy seed possess the gates of those which hate them.

Although the first rioters from the Preseli hills made further contributions to the destruction of the toll gates in Carmarthenshire in the 1840s, there is little further evidence of Thomas Rees's actual participation in the assaults.

His headstone in Bethel Chapel graveyard, erected in 1876, obviously makes no mention of his infamous past; it merely serves to remind us that however strong our ideals, however saintly or sinful our lives, we are all mortal.

ER COF AM

THOMAS REES
TRIAL OR PLWYF HWN
BU FARW MEDI 17, 1876.
YN 70 OED.
TWM CARNABWTH

Nid oes neb ond Duw yn gwybod
Beth a ddigwydd mewn diwornod.
Wrth gyrchu bresych at fy nginio
Daeth angau i fy ngardd i'm taro.

(No one but God knows what may happen in one day. While fetching a cabbage for my dinner, death came into my garden and struck me.)

Y Ceffyl Pren – The Wooden Horse

This was a well-known practice in south-west Wales – to make an offender (originally in sexual matters: adultery, fathering bastards or even wife-scolding) a total laughing stock within the local community. Often the victim, or an effigy, was paraded through the streets on a wooden pole or ladder, accompanied by a ribald description of the crime, delivered by men disguised in women's clothing.

> *Ran-dan-dan!*
> *Betty Bowen has beat her man.*
> *With what did she beat him, tell us now quick –*
> *Was't with a spoon or a walking stick?*
> *'Twas not with a rake or a milking stool*
> *But 'twas with a poker – she made her man fool!*

Later the wooden horse was used to hold to ridicule people who had 'betrayed the common folk', by conniving with the enemy – the turnpike owners and unjust landlords

In the byegone years it was a very fashionable kind of way to administer the functions of the law to its offenders, but since the county police was formed it has vanished away to oblivion . . .

. . . then a march was made headed by a band of the most discordant sounds in the whole creation composed of drums, tin pans, horns and such yells that it was ridiculous to the human ears, the castle (the guilty man's house) was taken and the prisoner being caught imploring for mercy but in such a plight no mercy on any ground could be obtained then he was tied on a ladder and carried on their shoulders to the village with great demonstrations. Afterwards he had to go through a great ordeal of being plunged into a deep pond but it was their custom to give a kind advice to all as well as to the prisoner prior to his immersion to the deep. Also due thought for his safety was secured by the aid of a few ploughlines attached to his chariot. One line was fastened to the front and the other attached to the steerage gear so he was pulled hither and thither at their own will . . . When the aforesaid punishment was administered to the individuals who were guilty of infringing the natural ties and the laws of conjugal rights (it) seemed at that period to be very effective in its purpose and mission.

(from an anonymous Pembrokeshire manuscript, dated 1899)

SARAH JACOB –

THE WELSH FASTING GIRL

Sarah Jacob, a young girl from Carmarthenshire, presents us with a problem. Was she saintly or sinful? Was she, as her father maintained, 'a gift from God', or was she merely a charlatan, egged on by her parents to become part of an elaborate, money-making freak show, which it must be admitted fooled a large part of the local population and the Victorian medical world?

Sarah Jacob, born in 1857, the third child of Evan Jacob and his wife Hannah, was by repute a precocious and intelligent child, who suffered a real but mysterious illness (possibly viral encephalitis) in the spring of 1867. This was treated by two local doctors, but to no avail. She stopped eating, and thus began the legend of 'The Welsh Fasting Girl'. Was food smuggled into her room by a sibling accomplice for the next two years? Did her parents act as willing partners in a deception? Was she indeed a miracle child? We shall never know.

It has been suggested that Sarah was a 'pioneer anorexic', but contemporary descriptions of her do not suggest an emaciated twelve-year-old. Other theories point to a manipulative, deeply disturbed, scheming child who knew how to gain attention and fame – by fasting and fitting – and thus prolong her childhood state, with no fear of being forced

into hard work or an early marriage. Perhaps it was a well-laid plan which went tragically wrong. In the end poor Sarah was forced to go along with her own deception, and starve herself to death, when confronted by a 24-hour strict nursing watch, based on a ten-point plan drawn up Dr J.J. Phillips from Guy's Hospital.

Her death was headline news. Christmas 1869 editions of *The Illustrated London News*, and *The Illustrated Police News* carried editorials, articles and artists' impressions, and even Charles Dickens speculated on the affair – of how an otherwise healthy child (since the post-mortem had revealed no signs of disease or abnormality) succumbed to such pain and suffering.

Who was to blame for her death? Some said the medical authorities, some Sarah herself, some blamed her parents. They were arrested and tried for manslaughter in Carmarthen, where the judge pressed for convictions on the grounds of parental neglect. Her father spent a year in Swansea gaol, her mother Hannah six months – but they eventually returned to the area in which the mysterious events had unfolded.

Saint or sinner, Sarah Jacob was certainly a major nineteenth-century Welsh tourist attraction. Her

SARAH JACOBS IN HER BED ROOM

story may now be half-forgotten, but in the late 1860s the railway station at Pencader (with its specially built refreshment booth) brought a daily stream of sightseers, doctors and reporters to 'the rather small old farmhouse … in a picturesque warm valley … where they found the girl, Sarah Jacob …', with rose petals strewn on her bed.

Right: Extracts from a letter written by Rev. Evan Jones, the Vicar of Llanifihangel-ar-arth, teacher and founder of the village school. Below: Sentencing of Evan and Hannah Jacob on manslaughter charges

19th February 1869
To the Editor of the Welshman

A STRANGE CASE

Sir,

Allow me to invite the attention of your readers to a most extraordinary case. Sarah Jacob, a little girl of twelve years of age and daughter of Mr Evan Jacob, Llethernevadd, in this parish, has not partaken of a single grain of food whatever during the last sixteen months. She did occasionally swallow a few drops of water during the first months of this period; but now she does not even do that . . . Medical men persist in saying that the thing is quite impossible, but all the nearest neighbours, who are thoroughly acquainted with the circumstances of the case, entertain no doubt whatever on the subject . . . would it not be worth their while for medical men to make an investigation into the nature of this strange case. Mr Evan Jacob would readily admit into his house any respectable person, who might be anxious to watch it, and see for himself . . .

Time Committed.	NAME.		Age.	Stature.	Complexion.	Where Born.
1870 March 15 Bailed same time	Evan Jacob Hannah Jacob		39 38	5 – 6¼ 5 – 1¾	Fresh Pale	Llanfihangelararth Ditto
No. 1364	Committed by.	Further Examination.	OFFENCE.		Time Tried.	Tried by.
	W P Lewes E.C.L Fitzwilliams and A H Jones Esquires		Manslaughter of Sarah Jacob "The Fasting Girl Case"		July 12 – 1870	Mr Justice Hanmen Assizes

Last Residence.	Single or Married.	No. of Children.	State of Instruction.	General Remarks.		Profession.
Llethernevadd Llanfihangelararth	M M	6	R & W. Imp. R. Welsh	Both surrendered in Court July 14. 1870		Farmer Wife of above Farmer
Original Sentence.		Present Sentence.		Hard Labour, Employed not being Hard Labour, or not Employed.	Whether in Custody before.	When Discharged.
12 C. m – H – L 6 C – m – H – L				H.L. Oakum.	No No	July 11.1871. From back Llan Jl. " Hannah Jacob Both from Swansea

SARAH JACOB 35

DIC PENDERYN

'A MARTYR OF THE WELSH WORKING CLASS'

Merthy Tydfil High Street c. 1850

Oh Lord, what an injustice!

(the dying words of Richard Lewis)

Centuries after the death of Tydfil the Martyr, another inhabitant of the same town met his death in a most shameful way. He was Richard Lewis (1808 – 1831) a young miner who was hanged in St Mary's Street Cardiff, wrongly convicted of an attack on a British soldier: he was the scapegoat for the Merthyr Rising.

In June 1831 the working people of Merthyr Tydfil, incensed by constant oppression, their harsh working conditions, cuts in wages and redundancies, rebelled against their landlords and employers. Rioting broke out in the streets when Bailiffs attempted to repossess goods owned by the unemployed and, in a desperate attempt to regain order, soldiers fired into the crowd outside the Castle Hotel. Sixteen of the mostly unarmed rioters were killed, but no soldiers received bullets wounds. However, Private Donald Black of the Highland Regiment, brought from Brecon as reinforcements, sustained a bayonet wound in the leg. Although the soldier was unable to identify his attacker, young Richard Lewis and his relative Lewis Lewis, with whom he was

lodging at the time in Penderyn, were arrested, tried and convicted. Lewis, a well-known troublemaker had his sentence commuted to transportation, (he'd shielded a Special Constable from the rioters, and the favour was repaid). Dic, however, was not so lucky. Despite repeated appeals for clemency, including an 11,000-signature petition from the people of Merthyr and intervention by a local Quaker ironmaster called Joseph T Price, his sentence was upheld by the Home Secretary, Lord Melbourne, well known for his severity when dealing with wrongdoers. Known colloquially as 'Dic Penderyn's whistle' the tipstaff or tipstave shown here belonged to the Special Constable who arrested Dic for the alleged attack on Private Donald Black. It has the words *Merthyr Tydfil* and the date *1831* inscribed on it, and would have contained the actual warrant for Richard Lewis's arrest. It can be seen in the South Wales Police Museum.

tip-staff (n): pl tip-staves – A staff tipped with metal: an officer who bears such a staff: a constable: a sheriff's officer.

In 1977 a memorial to Dic Penderyn, who had always remained a working class hero, was unveiled at Merthyr Tydfil public library by the general secretary of the TUC. At the ceremony, extracts from Alexander Cordell's popular novel about the Merthyr rising, called *The Fire People,* were read out. The famous Welsh songwriter Martyn Joseph also composed 'Dic Penderyn, the Ballad of Richard Lewis' as a testament to the injustice of the young man's trial and execution.

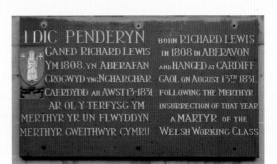

DIC PENDERYN
GANED RICHARD LEWIS YM 1808. yn ABERAFAN CROGWYD yngNGHARCHAR CAERDYDD ar AWST 13-1831. AR OL Y TERFYSG YM MERTHYR YR UN FLWYDDYN MERTHYR GWEITHWYR CYMRU

BORN RICHARD LEWIS IN 1808 in ABERAVON and HANGED at CARDIFF GAOL on AUGUST 13TH 1831. FOLLOWING THE MERTHYR INSURRECTION OF THAT YEAR A MARTYR OF THE WELSH WORKING CLASS

EXTRACT:

But louder and longer than the sound of guns
Is the memory of what was done;
You can only trample people down for so long,
Time will show you have not won.
And long before all this on a hill in Palestine
They strung another up they say was a friend of yours and mine
Dying in the place of another one,
But in the morning comes the sun.

Lift me up, oh lift me now,
Let me see the one I love;
Lift me up oh lift me now,
* let me see the one I love one more time.*

Martyn Joseph

(Popular reports of the day suggested that Dic's wife was heavily pregnant at the time, and had to be lifted above the crowds for a final view of her innocent husband)

The Cambrian newspaper carried almost daily reports on the trial proceedings and the ensuing actions of the Home Secretary, Lord Melbourne, who, despite continued calls for mercy, refused to stop the execution, having decided that he saw 'no grounds for mitigating the sentence.'

After Dic's death thousands of ordinary people followed the coffin as it was taken to his grave in Aberavon.

The apparent injustice only fuelled the decline in relations between the poor Welsh workers of the valleys and their rich and powerful employers – and the politicians of the day, who had been determined to teach the rebels a lesson they would not easily forget. Their inhumane treatment of the young miner created not an example to subdue unrest as they had intended (indeed, it furthered the cause of the Chartists and the early Trade

Unionists) but a folk hero of lasting affection – seen to champion the cause of the oppressed.

CONVICTED RIOTERS AT MERTHYR.
The public attention has been so much excited on the cases of the two prisoners sentenced to death at the late Cardiff Assizes, for crimes connected with the Merthyr riots, that we have taken pains to obtain authentic information as to the course which has been pursued, and which is likely to be pursued, with regard to both these misguided men, but particularly Richard Lewis, *alias* Dick Penderin, whose case appears to be one of peculiar interest, having given rise to the most extraordinary exertions on his behalf that were, perhaps, ever made by an individual on a similar occasion. We reported to our readers last week that a respite had arrived for Lewis Lewis (the huntsman), and that Richard had been left for execution. We stated that positive orders had been received to that effect; but in this we were misinformed, the fact being simply, that the law was left to take its course. The respite for Lewis Lewis was granted till the opinion of the Judge could be obtained by the authorities, and on Friday last the Deputy-Sheriff received a reprieve, so that this man's life is spared, and we trust the example of mercy will impress both his own mind and the minds of his associates beneficially. He will now be "transported beyond seas for the term of his natural life."—For Richard Lewis every appeal that had been made, as reported in our last, was made in vain. The decision of the Judge

PS: In 1874, a man called Ieuan Parker confessed on his deathbed to a priest in America, that he, not Dic Penderyn, had stabbed the young soldier. At least, this is what was reported in the *Western Mail*!

Coch Bach y Bala

THE GREAT ESCAPE

Ruthin Gaol

We are used to receiving postcards of seaside promenades and stately homes but it would be rather unusual to receive one featuring a coffin, or the exact spot where an escaped convict was apprehended. Yet these are views which the postman might have brought you in the autumn of 1913. Such was the fame of John Jones, nicknamed 'The Welsh Houdini' that his last days were immortalised for ever by a firm of postcard makers.

John Jones was born near Bala in the county of Merionethshire around 1853, and from an early age was involved in petty crime, stealing eggs and worthless property; he even boasted about fictitious crimes. By the time he was twenty he had already been in prison three times – a young man with a serious criminal record. By October 1879, when he was arrested for stealing fifteen watches, and sent to Ruthin Gaol to await trial, he had also spent time in prison for rioting in Bala (1878) and for being a rogue and a vagabond, 'loitering with intent to commit a felony' in a garden at Gresford (Chester Gaol 1879).

However, his imprisonment in Ruthin was short-lived, for the brazen criminal walked out of the main door whilst the staff were having supper, having opened four other doors on the way. He managed to remain free for several weeks, until he was recaptured in a bed in the Swan Inn, Mochdre near Colwyn Bay. Tradition states that he enjoyed relating his escapades to an audience – perhaps that is what happened in the public bar of the Swan, and the proposed £5 reward proved too much of a temptation for one of his listeners.

Although sentenced to 14 years' imprisonment (in either Dartmoor or Pentonville) Jones was back on the criminal circuit, released on licence, by 1891, when he once again found himself convicted of burglary. 'Coch Bach y Bala', or 'the Little Redhead of Bala' as he became known, was forever in and out of gaol. While awaiting transfer to Dartmoor from Caernarfon Gaol in 1900 he attempted an escape by breaking his loom to barricade the door and then tunnelling through the floor. In June 1913, only months after being released from a seven-year-stretch in Dartmoor, he was back in Bala cells, convicted of burglary at Jordan's the local solicitors, but he escaped again . . . and then again from Ruthin Gaol in September, while awaiting transfer to Stafford. But this was to be his last and fatal escape.

SENSATIONAL ESCAPE FROM RUTHIN PRISON ...
NOTED CRIMINAL'S LEAP FOR LIBERTY ...
HOLE CUT IN CELL WALL ...
IMPROVISED ROPE MADE FROM BEDCLOTHES.

John Jones, alias 'Little Turpin' and known throughout Wales as 'Coch Bach y Bala' affected his escape from Ruthin Prison on Tuesday morning, in a sensational manner, and at the time of writing is still at large. He gained his liberty as a result of indomitable pluck, great astuteness, and wonderful agility ... 'Coch Bach' is regarded by some as a hero; his performance is certainly a daring piece of work. The escape took place between four and five o'clock in the morning, before the majority of warders entered upon their duties ... the daring manner of his escape, and the quickness with which he left behind him the precincts of the prison baffled the gaol authorities and the police.

North Wales Times, 4 October 1913

After five days on the run, on the morning of 6th October 1913, Jones was shot in the woods near Nantclwyd Isaf by nineteen-year-old Reginald Jones-Bateman. He died of shock and haemorrhage from the wound in his leg. Jones-Bateman was later accused of manslaughter, but the charges were dropped. The image of 'Coch Bach' inserted into the woodland scene of the postcard was probably taken from his prison records.

John Jones was hardly a hero, and certainly not a saint – but in the popular imagination of the time, he was something of a celebrity. With so many escapes to his name, we can't help but admire his tenacity, and what the newspapers described as his 'indomitable pluck'. Everyone loves a lovable rogue, whether it be Norman Stanley Fletcher in *Porridge*, or Coch Bach y Bala, in Ruthin County Gaol!

Postcards of John Jones: the spot where he was shot and the subsequent burial

Acknowledgements

The author and publisher gratefully acknowledge the sources of the following images, and kind permission from those sources to publish here:

p.2: image of Saint Brynach by Janetta Turgel; p.4: Saint Silyn by Janetta Turgel; p.5: painting of Melangell by Jen Delyth (www.kelticdesigns.com); p.7: Pennant Melangell church by permission of The Saint Melangell Centre; p.8: photograph of statue of St David at Llanddewibrefi by Thomas Halliwell; p.10: 'A Song of the Western Road' by A.G. Prys-Jones first appeared in *Education Week 1925*, published by Pembrokeshire Education Committee; p.11: illustration by Nina K. Brisley taken from *Standard-bearers* by Elizabeth Clark (University of London Press, 1934); p.12 (top): by permission of St Mary's Church, Little Crosby; pp 12-15: photos of St Winefride's Well, Holywell by permission of the custodians; p.13: photo of stained glass window by permission of Jeffrey L. Thomas (www.castlewales.com); p.14: painting by Meryl Osse (mosseart.com); p.17: 'Murder of Tydfil' by Brett Breckon (www.brettbreckon.co.uk); p.18: drawing of Llanddona witch by Brett Breckon; p.20: painting of Bishop William Morgan by Keith Bowen for commemorative postage stamps, 1988; p.22: painting of Llanfihangel-y-Pennant by S. Maurice Jones, c.1891, by permission of Gwynedd Archives Service; p.23: photo of Mary Jones monument by Dyfed Elis-Gruffydd; p.24: photo of Twm Siôn Cati horseman at the Aberaeron Cob Festival pageant, by permission of Mark Pickthall; p.25: Twm Shon Catti cartoons which first appeared in the *Western Mail*; p.26: woodcut of Twm Siôn Cati, by permission of Powys Library Service, photo of Twm Siôn Cati's knife by permission of Carmarthen Museum Service; p.27: drawing of Madam Wen by Brett Breckon; photo of Rhosneigr beach by permission of Cyngor Sir Ynys Môn; p.28: illustration of sailing ship by Claudia Myatt; p.29: painting of Barti Ddu by Brett Breckon; p.31: detail from French Invasion Tapestry, Fishguard, by permission of Fishguard Invasion Centre Trust Ltd; p.32: illustration of Rebecca's daughters by Brett Breckon; p.35: court papers by permission of Carmarthen Archive Service; p.36: painting of Merthyr High Street by permission of Cyfarthfa Castle Museum; tip-staff by permission of South Wales Police Museum; p.37: song lyrics by permission of Martyn Joseph (www.martynjoseph.com); plaque and newspaper cutting by permission of Merthyr Tydfil Public Library; p.38-9: photos of Ruthin Gaol and of the funeral of Coch Bach y Bala by permission of Denbighshire Records Office

Inside back cover: Saints' frieze by Janetta Turgel

It has not been possible to trace the owner of copyright in every case. The publishers apologise for any omission and will be pleased to remedy any oversight when re-printing.